T O

_____

———ᘓᘓᘓ———

F R O M

_____

———ᘓᘓᘓ———

D A T E

_____

If You're Missing
BABYJESUS

*A True Story That Embraces
the Spirit of Christmas*

JEAN GIETZEN
ILLUSTRATIONS BY VICKIE SHUCK

Multnomah Publishers
SISTERS, OREGON

IF YOU'RE MISSING BABY JESUS
published by Multnomah Publishers, Inc.

© 1999 by Multnomah Publishers, Inc.
Illustrations © 1999 by Vicki Shuck
International Standard Book Number: 1-57673-498-6

Design by David Carlson Design

Multnomah is a trademark of Multnomah Publishers, Inc.,
and is registered in the U.S. Patent and Trademark Office.
The colophon is a trademark of Multnomah Publishers, Inc.

Printed in the United States of America

For information:
MULTNOMAH PUBLISHERS, INC.
POST OFFICE BOX 1720
SISTERS, OREGON 97759

Library of Congress Cataloging-in-Publication Data

Gietzen, Jean.
    If you're missing Baby Jesus / by Jean Gietzen.
        p.   cm.
    ISBN 1-57673-498-6 (alk. paper)
    1. Christmas—North dakota.   2. Gietzen, Jean   I. Title
    BV45.G49   1999
    263'.915—dc21

99 00 01 02 03 04 05 — 10 9 8 7 6 5 4 3 2

IN THE DEPTHS of a bitterly cold December, my mother decided it simply wouldn't do to go through the holidays without a nativity set.

It was 1943, in a small town in North Dakota. My father worked for an oil company during my growing-up years, and we'd moved around to several different parts of the state with his job. At some point between one move and another, we lost our family's little manger scene.

Happily, Mother found another at our local five and dime for only $3.99. When my brother and I helped her unpack the set, however, we found two figurines of the baby Jesus.

Mother frowned. "Someone must have packed this wrong," she said, counting out the pieces. "We have one

Joseph, one Mary, three wise men, three shepherds, two lambs, a donkey, a cow, an angel—and two babies. Oh, dear! I suppose some set down at the store is missing a baby Jesus."

"Hey, that's great, Mom," my brother said with a laugh. "Now we have twins!"

Mother wouldn't have a bit of it. "You two run right back down to the store and tell the manager that we have an extra Jesus."

"Ah, Mom."

"Go on with you now. Tell him to put a sign on the remaining boxes saying that if a set is missing a baby Jesus, call 7162."

She smiled. "I'll give you each a penny for some candy. And don't forget your mufflers. It's freezing cold out there."

The manager copied down my mother's message, and sure enough, the next time we were in the store we saw his cardboard sign:

If you're missing Baby Jesus, call 7162.

All week long we waited for the call to come. Surely, we thought, someone was missing that important figurine.

What was a nativity set without the main attraction? Each time the phone rang, my mother would say, "I'll bet that's about Jesus."

But it never was.

With increasing exasperation, my father tried to explain that the figurine could be missing from a set anywhere—Minot, Fargo, or even Walla Walla, Washington, for that matter. After all, packing errors occurred all the time. He suggested we just put the extra Jesus back in the box and forget about it.

"Back in the box!" I wailed. "What a terrible thing to do to the baby Jesus. And at Christmastime, too."

"Someone will surely call," my mother reasoned. "We'll just keep the babies together in the manger until we find the owner."

That made my brother and me happy. It was special to look into that little manger and see two Christ children, side by side, gazing up into the adoring eyes of Mary. And was that a surprised look on Joseph's face?

But the days went by, and no one called. When we still hadn't heard from anyone by five o'clock on

Christmas Eve, my mother insisted that Daddy "just run down to the store" to see if there were any sets left.

"You can see them right through the window, over on the counter," she said. "It they're all gone, I'll know someone is bound to call tonight."

"Run down to the store?" my father thundered. "Ethel, it's fifteen below zero out there!"

"Oh, Daddy," I said, "we'll go with you. Won't we, Tommy?" Tommy nodded vigorously. "We'll bundle up good. And...we can look at all the decorations on the way."

My father blew out a long sigh and headed for the front closet. "I can't believe I'm doing this," he muttered. "Every time the phone rings everybody yells at me to see if it's about Jesus. And now I'm going off on the coldest night of the year to peek in some store window to see if He's there or not there."

Daddy muttered all the way down the block in the cold, still air, while my brother and I raced each other to the store. The streets were empty and silent. But behind each lighted window, we knew that families were gathering around Christmas trees and manger scenes and

fireplaces and tables laden with tasty holiday treats.

I was the first to reach the store window, where colored lights flickered along the edge of the frosty pane. Pushing my nose up against the glass, I peered into the darkened store.

"They're all gone, Daddy!" I yelled. "Every set must be sold."

"Hooray!" my brother cheered, catching up with me. "The mystery will be solved tonight!"

My father, who had seen no logical reason to run, remained some yards behind us. When he heard our tidings, he turned on his heel and started for home.

Inside the house once more, we were surprised to see only one baby Jesus in the manger. Where was the Twin? For that matter, where was Mother? Had she vanished, too?

Daddy was unperturbed. "Someone must have called," he reasoned, pulling off his boots. "She must have gone out to deliver the figurine. You kids get busy stringing those popcorn strands for the tree, and I'll wrap your mother's present."

We had almost completed one strand when the phone rang. "You get it, Jean," my father called. "Tell 'em we already found a home for Jesus!"

My brother gave me a quick, eager look. Our mystery would be solved at last.

But the telephone call didn't solve any mystery at all. It created a much bigger one.

It was my mother on the phone, with instructions for us to come to 205 Chestnut Street immediately, and to bring three blankets, a box of cookies, and some milk.

My father was incredulous. "I can't believe this," he groaned, retrieving his boots for the second time that evening. "What in Sam Hill has she gotten us into?" He paused. "205 Chestnut. Why, that's eight blocks away. Wrap that milk up good in the blankets or it'll turn to ice by the time we get there. Why in the name of heaven can't we get on with Christmas? It's prob'ly twenty below out there now. And the wind's pickin' up. Of all the crazy things to do on a night like this."

Tommy and I didn't mind at all. It was Christmas Eve, and we were in the middle of an adventure. We sang

carols at the top of our lungs all the way to Chestnut Street. My father, carrying his bundle of blankets, milk, and cookies, looked for all the world like Saint Nicholas with his arms full of goodies.

My brother called back to him. "Hey Dad, let's pretend we're looking for a place to stay—just like Joseph 'n' Mary."

"Let's pretend we're in Bethlehem where it's probably sixty-five degrees in the shade right now," my father answered.

The house at 205 Chestnut turned out to be the darkest one on the block. One tiny light burned in the living room, and the moment we set foot on the front porch steps, my mother opened the door and shouted, "They're here, they're here! Oh, thank God you got here, Ray! You kids take those blankets into the living room and wrap up the little ones on the couch. I'll take the milk and cookies."

"Ethel, would you mind telling me what's going on here?" my father huffed. "We've just hiked through sub-zero weather with the wind in our faces all the way..."

"Never mind all that now," my mother interrupted. "There's no heat in this house, and this young mother doesn't know what to do. Her husband walked out on her. Those poor little children will have a very bleak Christmas, so don't you complain. I told her you could fix that oil furnace in a jiffy."

Well, that stopped my father right in his tracks.

My mother strode off to the kitchen to warm the milk, while my brother and I wrapped up the five little children who huddled together on the couch. The distraught young mother, wringing her hands, explained to my father that her husband had run off, taking bedding, clothing, and almost every piece of furniture. But she'd been doing all right, she explained, until the furnace broke down.

"I been doin' washin' and ironin' for folks, and cleanin' the five 'n' dime," she said. "I—I saw your number every day there, on those boxes on the counter. Then—when the furnace went out—that number kept goin' through my mind. 7162. 7162.

"Said on the box that if a person was missin' Jesus, they should call you. That's how I knew you was good

Christian people, willin' to help folks. I figured that maybe you'd help me, too. So I stopped at the grocery store tonight and called your missus. I'm not missin' Jesus, mister, because I surely love the Lord. But I am missin' heat.

"Me and the kids ain't got no beddin', and no warm clothes. I got a few Christmas toys for 'em, but I got no money to fix that furnace."

"It's okay," my father said gently. "You called the right number. Now, let's see here. You've got a little oil burner there in the dining room. Shouldn't be too hard to fix. Probably just a clogged flue. I'll look it over, see what it needs."

My mother came into the living room carrying a plate of cookies and a tray of cups with warm milk. As she set the cups down on the coffee table, I noticed the figure of the baby Jesus—our Twin—lying in the center of the table. There was no Mary or Joseph, no wise men or shepherds. Just Jesus.

The children stared wide-eyed with wonder at the plate of cookies my mother set before them. One of the littlest ones woke up and crawled out from under the blanket. Seeing all the strangers in his house, his face

puckered up, and he began to cry. My mother swooped him in her arms and began to sing to him.

"This, this, is Christ the King,
Whom shepherds guard and angels sing…"

Mother crooned, while the child wailed.

"Haste, haste, to bring Him laud,
the Babe, the son of Mary."

She went on singing, oblivious to the child's cries. She danced the baby around the room until finally, in spite of himself, he settled down again.

"You hear that, Chester?" the young woman said to another child. "That nice lady is singin' 'bout the Lord Jesus. He ain't ever gonna walk out on us. Why, He sent these people to us just to fix our furnace. And blankets— now we got blankets, too! Oh, we'll be warm tonight. Jesus saves, that's what He does."

My father, finishing his work on the oil burner, wiped his hands on his muffler. "I've got it going, ma'am, but you need more oil. I'll make a few calls tonight when I get home and we'll get you some.

"Yessir," he said with a sudden smile. "You called the right number."

When Daddy figured the furnace was going strong once more, our family bundled up and made our way home under a clear, starry heaven. My father didn't say a thing about the cold weather. I could tell he was turning things around in his mind all the way home. As soon as we set foot inside the front door, he strode over the telephone and dialed a number.

"Ed? This is Ray. How are ya? Yes, Merry Christmas to you, too. Say, Ed, we have kind of an unusual situation here tonight. I know you've got that pickup truck, and I was wonderin' if we could round up some of the boys and find a Christmas tree, you know, and a couple things for..."

The rest of the conversation was lost in a blur as my brother and I ran to our rooms and began pulling clothes out of our closets, and toys off our shelves.

My mother checked through our belongings for sizes, and selected some of the games she said "might do." Then she added some of her own sweaters and slacks to our stack.

It was a Christmas Eve like no other.

Instead of going to bed in a snug, warm house, dreaming of a pile of presents to open on Christmas morning, we were up way past our bedtime, wrapping gifts for a little family we'd only just met. The men my father had called found oil for the furnace, bedding, two chairs, and three lamps. They made two trips to 205 Chestnut before the night was done.

On the second trip, he let us go, too. Even though it must have been thirty below by then, my father let us ride in the back of the truck, with our gifts stacked all around us.

My brother's eyes danced in the starlight. Without saying anything, we both knew Christmas could never be the same after this. The extra Jesus in our home hadn't been ours to keep after all. He was for someone else...for a desperate family in a dark little house on Chestnut Street.

Someone who needed Jesus as much as we did.

And we got to take Him there.